Honey Bees and Hives

by Lola M. Schaefer

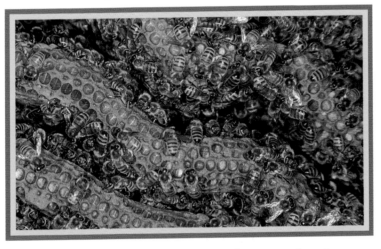

Consulting Editor: Gail Saunders-Smith, Ph.D.

Consultant: Troy Fore, Executive Director,
American Beekeeping Federation

Pebble Books

an imprint of Capstone Press
Mankato, Minnesota

Pebble Books are published by Capstone Press
818 North Willow Street, Mankato, Minnesota 56001
http://www.capstone-press.com

Library of Congress Cataloging-in-Publication Data
Schaefer, Lola M., 1950–
    Honey bees and hives/by Lola M. Schaefer.
    p. cm.—(Honey bees)
    Includes bibliographical references and index.
    Summary: Simple text and photographs introduce the life and work of
honeybees in hives.
    ISBN 0-7368-0230-4
    1. Honeybee—Juvenile literature. 2. Beehives—Juvenile literature. [1. Honeybee.
2. Bees. 3. Beehives.] I. Title. II. Series: Schaefer, Lola M., 1950–   Honey bees.
QL568.A6S283   1999
595.79'9—dc21
                                                                98-40907
                                                                CIP
                                                                AC

Note to Parents and Teachers

The Honey Bees series supports national science standards for units on the diversity and unity of life. The series also shows that animals have features that help them live in different environments. This book describes and illustrates types of honey bee hives and honey bee activities within hives. The photographs support early readers in understanding the text. The repetition of words and phrases helps early readers learn new words. This book also introduces early readers to subject-specific vocabulary words, which are defined in the Words to Know section. Early readers may need assistance to read some words and to use the Table of Contents, Words to Know, Read More, Internet Sites, and Index/Word List sections of the book.

Table of Contents

Hives 5
Working in Hives 11

Note to Parents and Teachers . . . 2
Words to Know 22
Read More 23
Internet Sites 23
Index/Word List 24

4

Honey bees live in hives.

Some honey bees build
hives in trees.

Some honey bees live in hives that beekeepers build.

10

Honey bees build honeycombs in hives.

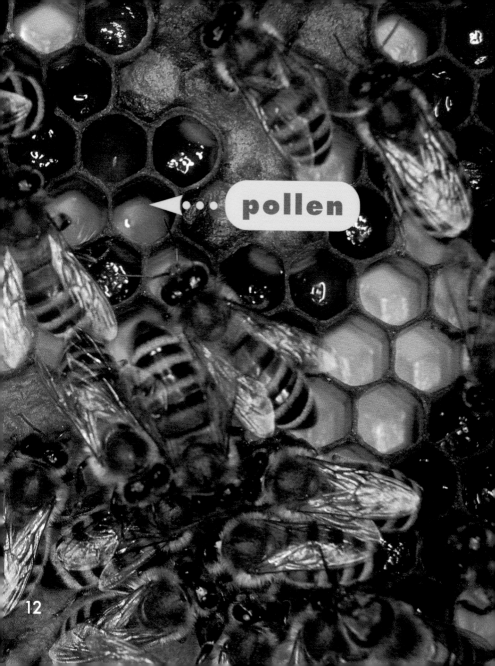

Honey bees store pollen in hives.

14

Honey bees make honey
in hives.

egg ••••➤

Honey bees lay eggs
in hives.

young
honey
bee

18

Honey bees feed young honey bees in hives.

Honey bees guard
their hives.

Words to Know

beekeeper—a person who raises honey bees and gathers honey from the hives

egg—a small case in which a young bee forms; only queen honey bees lay eggs; each hive has only one queen honey bee.

guard—to protect a place; honey bees guard their hives to keep out enemies such as bears, spiders, and other bees.

hive—a structure where honey bees live; thousands of honey bees live in a hive.

honey—a sweet, sticky matter that honey bees make; honey bees make honey out of nectar.

honeycomb—a group of wax cells in which honey bees store pollen, nectar, honey, and eggs; worker bees build honeycombs.

pollen—tiny, yellow grains in flowers; honey bees eat pollen.

store—to save or put away; honey bees store pollen in their hives.

Read More

Crewe, Sabrina. *The Bee.* Life Cycles. Austin, Texas: Raintree Steck-Vaughn, 1997.

Holmes, Kevin J. *Bees.* Animals. Mankato, Minn.: Bridgestone Books, 1998.

Shaw, Nancy J. *Bee.* Mankato, Minn.: Creative Education, 1998.

Internet Sites

Bee Basics
http://www.roctronics.com/BEE-BASE.HTM

Games and Puzzles
http://grizzly.umt.edu/biology/bees/games.htm

John's Beekeeping Notebook
http://home.earthlink.net/~jcaldeira/beekeeping/obs1.htm

Index/Word List

beekeepers, 9
build, 7, 9, 11
eggs, 17
feed, 19
guard, 21
hives, 5, 7, 9,
  11, 13, 15, 17,
  19, 21
honey, 15

honey bees,
  5, 7, 9, 11, 13, 15,
  17, 19, 21
honeycombs, 11
lay, 17
pollen, 13
store, 13
trees, 7
young, 19

Word Count: 58
Early-Intervention Level: 8

Editorial Credits

Martha E. Hillman, editor; Steve Weil/Tandem Design, cover designer and illustrator; Kim Danger and Sheri Gosewisch, photo researchers

Photo Credits

Craig D. Wood, 14, 18
James H. Robinson, cover
Lynn M. Stone, 4
McDaniel Photography/Stephen McDaniel, 1, 10, 12, 16
Phillip Roullard, 6
Scott Camazine, 20
Uniphoto/Mellott, 8